Campbell's

CLASSIC
RECIPES

Publications International, Ltd.

Every recipe was developed and tested in the Campbell Soup Company Global
Consumer Food Center by professional home economists.

"Campbell's," "Healthy Request," "Swanson," "Pace," "Prego," "Franco-
American," "V8" and "V8 Splash" are registered trademarks used with
permission by Campbell Soup Company. "Pepperidge Farm" is a registered
trademark used with permission by Pepperidge Farm, Incorporated.

Front cover photography by Campbell Soup Company Creative Photography
Studio.

All other photography:
Photography: Sacco Studio Limited, Chicago
Photographer: Tom O'Connell
Photo Stylist: Paula M. Walters
Food Stylists: Gail O'Donnell, Dianne Hugh
Assistant Food Stylist: Liza Brown

Pictured on the front cover *(clockwise from top):* Green Bean Bake *(page 24)*,
Mom's Best Gravy *(page 30)* and Skinny Mashed Potatoes *(page 31)*.

Pictured on the back cover *(left to right):* Turkey Primavera *(page 74)* and
No-Guilt Chicken Pot Pie *(page 44)*.

ISBN: 0-7853-3554-4

Manufactured in U.S.A.

8 7 6 5 4 3 2 1

Nutritional Analysis: Values are approximate; calculations are based upon food
composition data in the Campbell Soup Company Master Data Base. Some
variation in nutrition values may result from periodic product changes. Each
analysis is based on the food items in the ingredient list, excluding optional
ingredients and garnishes. When a choice is given for an ingredient, calculations
are based upon the first choice listed.

Microwave Cooking: Microwave ovens vary in wattage. Use the cooking times
as guidelines and check for doneness before adding more time.

Preparation/Cooking Times: Preparation times are based on the approximate
amount of time required to assemble the recipe before cooking, baking or
chilling. These times include preparation steps such as measuring, chopping and
mixing. The fact that some preparations and cooking can be done simultaneously
is taken into account. Preparation of optional ingredients and serving suggestions
is not included.

Campbell's

CLASSIC
RECIPES

APPETIZERS & SWEETS

Stuffed Clams

Prep Time: 35 minutes   **Cook Time:** 20 minutes

- 24 cherrystone clams, scrubbed
- 2 slices bacon, diced
- 3 tablespoons margarine *or* butter
- 1 medium onion, chopped (about ½ cup)
- ¼ teaspoon garlic powder *or* 2 cloves garlic, minced
- 1½ cups PEPPERIDGE FARM Herb Seasoned Stuffing
- 2 tablespoons grated Parmesan cheese
- 2 tablespoons chopped fresh parsley *or* 2 teaspoons dried parsley flakes

1. Open clams. Remove and discard top shell. Arrange clams in large shallow baking pan.

2. In medium skillet over medium heat, cook bacon until crisp. Remove and drain on paper towels.

3. Add margarine, onion and garlic powder to hot drippings and cook until tender. Add stuffing, cheese, parsley and bacon. Mix lightly. Spoon on top of each clam. Bake at 400°F. for 20 minutes or until clams are done.   *Makes 24 appetizers*

Clockwise from top left: *Sausage Stuffed Mushrooms (page 8), Stuffed Clams and Savory Criss-Cross Pastry (page 13)*

Sausage Stuffed Mushrooms

(photo on page 7)

Prep Time: 25 minutes   **Cook Time:** 10 minutes

24 medium mushrooms (about 1 pound)
 2 tablespoons margarine *or* butter, melted
¼ pound bulk pork sausage
 1 cup PACE Picante Sauce *or* Thick & Chunky Salsa
½ cup dry bread crumbs
   Chopped fresh cilantro *or* parsley

1. Remove stems from mushrooms. Chop enough stems to make *1 cup* and set aside. Brush mushroom caps with margarine and place top-side down in shallow baking pan. Set aside.

2. In medium skillet over medium-high heat, cook sausage and chopped mushroom stems until sausage is browned, stirring to separate meat.

3. Add *½ cup* picante sauce and bread crumbs. Mix lightly. Spoon about *1 tablespoon* stuffing mixture into each mushroom cap.

4. Bake at 425°F. for 10 minutes or until mushrooms are heated through. Top each with *1 teaspoon* remaining picante sauce and cilantro.   *Makes 24 appetizers*

Tip

To make ahead, prepare through step 3. Cover and refrigerate up to 24 hours. Bake as in step 4.

Spinach-Cheese Swirls

(photo on page 11)
Thaw Time: 30 minutes
Prep Time: 20 minutes   **Cook Time:** 15 minutes

½ package (17¼-ounce size) **PEPPERIDGE FARM**
    Frozen Puff Pastry Sheets (1 sheet)
1 egg
1 tablespoon water
½ cup shredded Muenster *or* Monterey Jack cheese
    (2 ounces)
¼ cup grated Parmesan cheese
1 green onion, chopped (about 2 tablespoons)
⅛ teaspoon garlic powder
1 package (about 10 ounces) frozen chopped
    spinach, thawed and *well drained*

1. Thaw pastry sheet at room temperature 30 minutes. Preheat oven to 400°F. Mix egg and water and set aside. Mix Muenster cheese, Parmesan cheese, onion and garlic powder. Set aside.

2. Unfold pastry on lightly floured surface. Brush with egg mixture. Top with cheese mixture and spinach. Starting at one side, roll up like a jelly roll. Cut into 20 (½-inch) slices. Place 2 inches apart on baking sheet. Brush tops with egg mixture.

3. Bake 15 minutes or until golden.   *Makes 20 appetizers*

Tip
To thaw spinach, microwave on HIGH 3 minutes, breaking apart with fork halfway through heating.

Ham and Broccoli Swirls

Thaw Time: 30 minutes
Prep Time: 20 minutes   **Cook Time:** 15 minutes

½ package (17¼-ounce size) PEPPERIDGE FARM
    Frozen Puff Pastry Sheets (1 sheet)
1 egg
1 tablespoon water
1 container (4 ounces) whipped cream cheese with
    chives spread
1 package (10 ounces) frozen chopped broccoli
    (2 cups), thawed and *well drained*
1 cup finely chopped cooked ham

1. Thaw pastry sheet at room temperature 30 minutes. Preheat oven to 400°F. Mix egg and water and set aside.

2. Unfold pastry on lightly floured surface. Roll into 16- by 12-inch rectangle. Spread cream cheese over rectangle to within ½ inch of edges. Top with broccoli and ham. Starting at long side, roll up like a jelly roll, only to center. Roll up opposite side to center. Brush between rolls with egg mixture, then gently press rolls together.

3. Cut into 32 (½-inch) slices. Place 2 inches apart on greased baking sheet. Brush tops with egg mixture.

4. Bake 15 minutes or until golden. Serve warm or at room temperature. *Makes 32 appetizers*

Tip

To make ahead, prepare through step 3. Freeze. When frozen, store in plastic bag up to 1 month. To bake, preheat oven to 400°F. Place frozen slices on baking sheet. Bake 20 minutes or until golden.

Clockwise from top: Parmesan Cheese Crisps (page 12), Spinach-Cheese Swirls (page 9) and Ham and Broccoli Swirls

Parmesan Cheese Crisps

(photo on page 11)
Thaw Time: 30 minutes
Prep Time: 20 minutes   **Cook Time:** 10 minutes

½ package (17¼-ounce size) PEPPERIDGE FARM
    Frozen Puff Pastry Sheets (1 sheet)
1 egg
1 tablespoon water
¼ cup grated Parmesan cheese
1 tablespoon chopped fresh parsley *or* 1 teaspoon
    dried parsley flakes
½ teaspoon dried oregano leaves, crushed

1. Thaw pastry sheet at room temperature 30 minutes. Preheat oven to 400°F. Mix egg and water and set aside. Mix cheese, parsley and oregano and set aside.

2. Unfold pastry on lightly floured surface. Roll into 14- by 10-inch rectangle. Cut in half lengthwise. Brush both halves with egg mixture. Top 1 rectangle with cheese mixture. Place remaining rectangle over cheese-topped rectangle, egg-side down. Roll gently with rolling pin to seal.

3. Cut crosswise into 28 (½-inch) strips. Twist strips and place 2 inches apart on greased baking sheet, pressing down ends. Brush with egg mixture.

4. Bake 10 minutes or until golden. Serve warm or at room temperature.   *Makes 28 appetizers*

Tip

To make ahead, twist strips. Place on baking sheet and brush with egg mixture. Freeze. When frozen, store in plastic bag for up to 1 month. To bake, preheat oven to 400°F. Place frozen strips on greased baking sheet. Bake 15 minutes or until golden.

Savory Criss-Cross Pastry

(photo on page 7)
Thaw Time: 30 minutes
Prep Time: 20 minutes   **Cook Time:** 35 minutes

- ½ package (17¼-ounce size) **PEPPERIDGE FARM Frozen Puff Pastry Sheets (1 sheet)**
- 2 **eggs**
- 1 **tablespoon water**
- ½ **pound bulk pork sausage**
- 1 cup **PEPPERIDGE FARM Herb Seasoned Stuffing**
- 1 **small onion, chopped (about ¼ cup)**
- 1 **cup chopped mushrooms (about 3 ounces)**

1. Thaw pastry sheet at room temperature 30 minutes. Preheat oven to 375°F. Mix **1** egg and water and set aside.

2. Mix sausage, stuffing, remaining egg, onion and mushrooms *thoroughly.*

3. Unfold pastry on lightly floured surface. Cut slits 1 inch apart from outer edge up to fold mark on each side of pastry. Spoon sausage mixture down center of pastry. Starting at one end, fold pastry strips over stuffing mixture, alternating sides, to cover sausage mixture. Place on baking sheet. Brush with egg mixture.

4. Bake 35 minutes or until golden. Slice and serve warm.
Serves 4 as a main dish or 8 as an appetizer

Caramel Apple Tarts

Thaw Time: 30 minutes

Prep Time: 20 minutes   **Cook Time:** 25 minutes

   1 package (10 ounces) PEPPERIDGE FARM Frozen
      Puff Pastry Shells
   6 tablespoons sugar
   ½ teaspoon ground cinnamon
   ½ teaspoon ground ginger
   3 apples *or* pears, peeled, cored and thinly sliced
      (about 4 cups)
  ⅔ cup caramel sauce
     Vanilla ice cream

1. Thaw pastry shells at room temperature 30 minutes. Preheat oven to 375°F. Mix sugar, cinnamon and ginger and set aside.

2. Roll pastry shells into 5-inch circles on lightly floured surface. Place on 2 shallow-sided baking sheets. Divide apple slices among pastry circles. Sprinkle each with *1 tablespoon* sugar mixture. Bake 25 minutes or until pastry is golden.

3. In small saucepan over medium heat, heat caramel sauce until warm. Spoon over tarts. Serve with ice cream.   *Serves 6*

Tip

For more delicious PEPPERIDGE FARM Puff Pastry recipes and ideas, visit our Web site at www.puffpastry.com

Left to right: *Caramel Apple Tarts and Apple Strudel (page 19)*

Lemon Meringue Tarts

Bake Time: 30 minutes
Prep Time: 20 minutes   **Cook Time:** 15 minutes

1 package (10 ounces) PEPPERIDGE FARM Frozen
    Puff Pastry Shells
1 package (3 ounces) lemon pudding mix
1 teaspoon grated lemon peel
2 egg whites
¼ cup sugar

1. Bake and cool pastry shells according to package directions.

2. Prepare pudding mix according to package directions for pie filling. Stir in lemon peel and cool to room temperature.

3. Spoon about ⅓ *cup* pudding into each pastry shell. Preheat oven to 325°F.

4. In medium bowl place egg whites. Beat with electric mixer at high speed until frothy. Gradually add sugar, beating until soft peaks form. Spoon over pudding sealing edges. Place on baking sheet. Bake 12 minutes or until lightly browned. Remove from baking sheet and cool on wire rack.

Serves 6

Variation: Substitute sweetened whipped cream **or** whipped topping for egg whites and sugar. Top each filled pastry shell with whipped cream. Garnish with lemon slices if desired. Serve immediately or cover and refrigerate until serving time.

Top to bottom: *Southern Pecan Crisps (page 18) and Lemon Meringue Tarts*

Southern Pecan Crisps

(photo on page 17)
Thaw Time: 30 minutes
Prep Time: 25 minutes   **Cook Time:** 12 minutes

> ½ package (17¼-ounce size) **PEPPERIDGE FARM**
>   **Frozen Puff Pastry Sheets (1 sheet)**
> ½ **cup packed brown sugar**
> 2 **tablespoons margarine** *or* **butter, melted**
> ⅓ **cup chopped pecans**
>   **Confectioners' sugar**

1. Thaw pastry sheet at room temperature 30 minutes. Preheat oven to 400°F. Mix brown sugar, margarine and pecans and set aside.

2. Unfold pastry on lightly floured surface. Roll into 15- by 12-inch rectangle. Cut into 20 (3-inch) squares. Press squares into bottoms of 3-inch muffin-pan cups. Place **1 heaping teaspoon** pecan mixture in center of each.

3. Bake 12 minutes or until golden. Remove from pans. Cool on wire rack. Sprinkle with confectioners' sugar.

Makes 20 pastries

Tip

Wrap unused pastry sheets in plastic wrap or foil and return to the freezer. Thawed pastry sheets will be cool to the touch and will unfold without breaking. Thawed pastry sheets can be refrigerated up to 2 days.

Apple Strudel

(photo on page 15)
Thaw Time: 30 minutes
Prep Time: 30 minutes   **Cook Time:** 35 minutes

½ package (17¼-ounce size) PEPPERIDGE FARM
    Frozen Puff Pastry Sheets (1 sheet)
1 egg
1 tablespoon water
2 tablespoons sugar
1 tablespoon all-purpose flour
¼ teaspoon ground cinnamon
2 large Granny Smith apples, peeled, cored and
    thinly sliced (about 3 cups)
2 tablespoons raisins

1. Thaw pastry sheet at room temperature 30 minutes. Preheat oven to 375°F. Mix egg and water and set aside. Mix sugar, flour and cinnamon. Add apples and raisins and toss to coat. Set aside.

2. Unfold pastry on lightly floured surface. Roll into 16- by 12-inch rectangle. With short side facing you, spoon apple mixture on bottom half of pastry to within 1 inch of edges. Starting at short side, roll up like a jelly roll. Place seam-side down on baking sheet. Tuck ends under to seal. Brush with egg mixture. Cut several 2-inch-long slits 2 inches apart on top.

3. Bake 35 minutes or until golden. Cool on baking sheet on wire rack 30 minutes. Slice and serve warm. Sprinkle with confectioners' sugar if desired.

Serves 6

Variation: Omit raisins.

Chocolate Mousse Napoleons with Strawberries & Cream

Thaw Time: 30 minutes
Prep Time: 25 minutes   **Cook Time:** 15 minutes

- ½ package (17¼-ounce size) PEPPERIDGE FARM Frozen Puff Pastry Sheets (1 sheet)
- 1 cup heavy cream
- ¼ teaspoon ground cinnamon
- 1 package (6 ounces) semi-sweet chocolate pieces, melted and cooled
- 2 cups sweetened whipped cream *or* whipped topping
- 1½ cups sliced strawberries
- 1 square (1 ounce) semi-sweet chocolate, melted (optional)
- Confectioners' sugar

1. Thaw pastry sheet at room temperature 30 minutes. Preheat oven to 400°F.

2. Unfold pastry on lightly floured surface. Cut into 3 strips along fold marks. Cut each strip into 6 rectangles.

3. Bake 15 minutes or until golden. Remove from baking sheet and cool on wire rack.

4. In medium bowl place cream and cinnamon. Beat with electric mixer at high speed until stiff peaks form. Fold in melted chocolate pieces. Split pastries into 2 layers. Spread 12 rectangles with chocolate cream. Top with another rectangle. Spread with whipped cream, sliced strawberries and remaining rectangles. Serve immediately or cover and refrigerate up to 4 hours. Just before serving, drizzle with melted chocolate and sprinkle with confectioners' sugar.   *Makes 12 napoleons*

Chocolate Mousse Napoleons with Strawberries & Cream

Glazed Carrot Raisin Cupcakes

Prep Time: 10 minutes   **Cook Time:** 20 minutes
Cool Time: 20 minutes

> 1 package spice cake mix (about 18 ounces)
> 1 can (10¾ ounces) CAMPBELL'S HEALTHY REQUEST
>   Condensed Tomato Soup
> ½ cup water
> 2 eggs
> 1 medium carrot, shredded (about ½ cup)
> ½ cup raisins
> 1 cup confectioners' sugar
> 3 tablespoons unsweetened apple juice

1. Preheat oven to 350°F. Place liners in 24 (2½-inch) muffin-pan cups. Set aside.

2. Mix cake mix, soup, water and eggs according to package directions. Fold in carrot and raisins. Spoon batter into cups, filling almost full.

3. Bake 20 minutes or until toothpick inserted in center comes out clean. Remove from pan and cool completely on wire rack.

4. Mix sugar and juice until smooth. Frost cupcakes.

Makes 24 cupcakes

Nutritional Values per Serving: Calories 124, Total Fat 2g, Saturated Fat 0g, Cholesterol 18mg, Sodium 182mg, Total Carbohydrate 24g, Protein 1g

Glazed Carrot Raisin Cupcakes

Campbell's
HOLIDAY TABLE TRADITIONS

Green Bean Bake

Prep Time: 10 minutes   **Cook Time:** 30 minutes

- 1 can (10¾ ounces) CAMPBELL'S Condensed Cream of Mushroom Soup *or* 98% Fat Free Cream of Mushroom Soup
- ½ cup milk
- 1 teaspoon soy sauce
  Dash pepper
- 4 cups cooked cut green beans
- 1 can (2.8 ounces) French fried onions (1⅓ cups)

1. In 1½-quart casserole mix soup, milk, soy sauce, pepper, beans and ½ *can* onions.

2. Bake at 350°F. for 25 minutes or until hot.

3. Stir. Sprinkle remaining onions over bean mixture. Bake 5 minutes more or until onions are golden.   *Serves 6*

Tip: Use 1 bag (16 to 20 ounces) frozen green beans, 2 packages (9 ounces *each*) frozen green beans, 2 cans (about 16 ounces *each*) green beans *or* about 1½ pounds fresh green beans for this recipe.

Green Bean Bake

Holiday Turkey with Apple Pecan Stuffing

Prep Time: 30 minutes   **Cook Time:** 4½ to 5 hours
Stand Time: 10 minutes

¼ cup margarine *or* butter
2 stalks celery, chopped (about 1 cup)
1 large onion, chopped (about 1 cup)
2 cans (10½ ounces *each*) CAMPBELL'S Condensed
   Chicken Broth
1 bag (14 ounces) PEPPERIDGE FARM Cubed Herb
   Seasoned Stuffing
2 medium apples, cored and chopped (about 2 cups)
1 cup chopped pecans
1 (12- to 14-pound) turkey
Vegetable oil

1. In large saucepan over medium heat, heat margarine. Add celery and onion and cook until tender. Add broth. Heat to a boil. Remove from heat. Add stuffing, apples and pecans. Mix lightly.

2. Remove package of giblets and neck from turkey cavity. Rinse turkey with cold water and pat dry. Spoon stuffing lightly into neck and body cavities.* Fold loose skin over stuffing. Tie ends of drumsticks together. Place turkey, breast side up, on rack in shallow roasting pan. Brush with oil. Insert meat thermometer into thickest part of meat, not touching bone.

3. Roast at 325°F. for 4½ to 5 hours or until thermometer reads 180°F., drumstick moves easily, and center of stuffing reaches 165°F., basting occasionally with pan drippings. Begin checking doneness after 4 hours roasting time. Allow turkey to stand 10 minutes before slicing.   *Serves 12 to 16*

Bake any remaining stuffing in covered casserole with turkey 30 minutes or until hot.

Variation: Omit apples and pecans.

Top to bottom: *Holiday Turkey with Apple Pecan Stuffing, Mom's Best Gravy (page 30) and Creamy Vegetable Medley (page 38)*

Sausage Corn Bread Stuffing

Prep Time: 15 minutes   **Cook Time:** 25 minutes

    ¼ pound bulk pork sausage
    1¼ cups water
     1 tablespoon chopped fresh parsley *or* 1 teaspoon
        dried parsley flakes
    ½ cup cooked whole kernel corn
    ½ cup shredded Cheddar cheese (2 ounces)
     4 cups PEPPERIDGE FARM Corn Bread Stuffing

1. In large saucepan over medium-high heat, cook sausage until browned, stirring to separate meat. Pour off fat.

2. Stir in water, parsley, corn and cheese. Add stuffing. Mix lightly. Spoon into greased 1½-quart casserole.

3. Cover and bake at 350°F. for 25 minutes or until hot.

Serves 6

Tip

This stuffing bake brings a new flavor to the traditional holiday meal—and is easy enough for an everyday meal!

Top to bottom: *Sausage Corn Bread Stuffing and Scalloped Apple Bake (page 34)*

Mom's Best Gravy

(photo on cover and page 27)
Prep Time: 5 minutes   **Cook Time:** 5 minutes

**2 cans (10½ ounces *each*) FRANCO-AMERICAN
   Turkey Gravy
6 tablespoons turkey pan drippings
¼ teaspoon pepper
⅛ teaspoon sage
   Hot mashed potatoes**

In small saucepan mix gravy, drippings, pepper and sage. Over medium heat, heat through. Serve over mashed potatoes.

Makes 2½ cups

Mushroom-Herb Gravy: Heat 6 tablespoons turkey drippings in large saucepan. Add 1 cup sliced mushrooms and ¼ teaspoon dried thyme leaves, crushed, and cook until mushrooms are tender. Add 2 cans (10½ ounces *each*) FRANCO-AMERICAN Turkey Gravy and heat through.

Sautéed Garlic & Onion Gravy: Heat 6 tablespoons turkey drippings in large saucepan. Add 1 cup chopped onion and 2 cloves garlic, minced, and cook until onion is tender. Add 2 cans (10½ ounces *each*) FRANCO-AMERICAN Turkey Gravy and heat through.

Tip

Didn't roast a turkey? Just substitute 2 tablespoons vegetable oil for the turkey drippings.

Skinny Mashed Sweet Potatoes

(photo on page 33)

Prep Time: 10 minutes   **Cook Time:** 15 minutes

> 2 cans (14½ ounces *each*) SWANSON Chicken Broth
>   (3½ cups)
> 4 large sweet potatoes *or* yams, peeled and cut into
>   1-inch pieces (about 7½ cups)
> Generous dash pepper
> 2 tablespoons packed brown sugar

1. In medium saucepan place broth and potatoes. Over high heat, heat to a boil. Reduce heat to medium. Cover and cook 10 minutes or until potatoes are tender. Drain, reserving broth.

2. Mash potatoes with *1¼ cups* broth and pepper. If needed, add additional broth until potatoes are desired consistency. Add brown sugar.   *Serves about 6*

Note: 1g fat per serving

Skinny Mashed Potatoes: Substitute 5 large potatoes, cut into 1-inch pieces (about 7½ cups) for sweet potatoes and omit brown sugar.
Note: ½g fat per serving (traditional mashed potato recipe: 8g fat per serving)

Skinny Garlic Mashed Potatoes: *(photo on page 41)* Substitute 2 cans (14½ ounces **each**) SWANSON Seasoned Chicken Broth with Roasted Garlic for Chicken Broth and 5 large potatoes, cut into 1-inch pieces, for sweet potatoes. Omit brown sugar.

Bye Bye Butter Stuffing

Prep Time: 10 minutes   **Cook Time:** 15 minutes

> 1 can (14½ ounces) SWANSON Chicken Broth
>   (1¾ cups)
>   Generous dash pepper
> 1 stalk celery, coarsely chopped (about ½ cup)
> 1 small onion, coarsely chopped (about ¼ cup)
> ½ cup sliced mushrooms (optional)
> 4 cups PEPPERIDGE FARM Herb Seasoned Stuffing

1. In medium saucepan mix broth, pepper, celery, onion and mushrooms. Over high heat, heat to a boil. Reduce heat to low. Cover and cook 5 minutes or until vegetables are tender.

2. Add stuffing. Mix lightly.   *Serves 5*

Note: 2g fat per serving (traditional stuffing recipe: 10g fat per serving)

Roasted Turkey Pan Gravy

Prep Time: 5 minutes   **Cook Time:** 10 minutes

> 1 can (14½ ounces) SWANSON Chicken Broth
>   (1¾ cups)
> 3 tablespoons all-purpose flour

Remove turkey from roasting pan. Pour off fat. In roasting pan gradually mix broth into flour. Over medium heat, cook until mixture boils and thickens, stirring constantly.   *Serves about 4*

Note: ½g fat per serving (traditional turkey gravy recipe: 8g fat per serving)

Clockwise from top: *Skinny Mashed Sweet Potatoes (page 31), Roasted Turkey Pan Gravy and Bye Bye Butter Stuffing*

Scalloped Apple Bake

(photo on page 29)

Prep Time: 25 minutes   **Cook Time:** 40 minutes

¼ cup margarine *or* butter, melted
¼ cup sugar
2 teaspoons grated orange peel
1 teaspoon ground cinnamon
1½ cups PEPPERIDGE FARM Corn Bread Stuffing
½ cup coarsely chopped pecans
1 can (16 ounces) whole berry cranberry sauce
⅓ cup orange juice *or* water
4 large cooking apples, cored and thinly sliced
(about 6 cups)

1. Lightly mix margarine, sugar, orange peel, cinnamon, stuffing and pecans and set aside.

2. Mix cranberry sauce, juice and apples. Add **half** the stuffing mixture. Mix lightly. Spoon into 8-inch square baking dish. Sprinkle remaining stuffing mixture over apple mixture.

3. Bake at 375°F. for 40 minutes or until apples are tender.

Serves 6

Tip

To melt margarine, remove wrapper and place in microwave-safe cup. Cover and microwave on HIGH 45 seconds.

Vegetable Stuffing Bake

(photo on page 37)
Prep Time: 15 minutes   **Cook Time:** 35 minutes

>   4 cups PEPPERIDGE FARM Herb Seasoned Stuffing
>   2 tablespoons margarine *or* butter, melted
>   1 can (10¾ ounces) CAMPBELL'S Condensed Cream
>   of Mushroom Soup *or* 98% Fat Free Cream of
>   Mushroom Soup
>   ½ cup sour cream
>   2 small zucchini, shredded (about 2 cups)
>   2 medium carrots, shredded (about 1 cup)
>   1 small onion, finely chopped (about ¼ cup)

1. Mix *1 cup* stuffing and margarine. Set aside.

2. Mix soup, sour cream, zucchini, carrots and onion. Add remaining stuffing. Mix lightly. Spoon into 1½-quart casserole. Sprinkle with reserved stuffing mixture.

3. Bake at 350°F. for 35 minutes or until hot.   *Serves 6*

Creamed Onion Bake

Prep Time: 15 minutes   **Cook Time:** 30 minutes

    4 tablespoons margarine *or* butter
1½ cups PEPPERIDGE FARM Corn Bread Stuffing
    2 tablespoons chopped fresh parsley *or* 2 teaspoons
        dried parsley flakes
    3 large onions, cut in half and sliced (about 3 cups)
    1 can (10¾ ounces) CAMPBELL'S Condensed Cream
        of Mushroom Soup *or* 98% Fat Free Cream of
        Mushroom Soup
  ¼ cup milk
    1 cup frozen peas
    1 cup shredded Cheddar cheese (4 ounces)

1. Melt *2 tablespoons* margarine and mix with stuffing and parsley.
Set aside.

2. In medium skillet over medium heat, heat remaining margarine.
Add onions and cook until tender.

3. Stir in soup, milk and peas. Spoon into 2-quart shallow baking
dish. Sprinkle cheese and stuffing mixture over soup mixture.

4. Bake at 350°F. for 30 minutes or until hot.   *Serves 6*

Top to bottom: *Vegetable Stuffing Bake (page 35)*
and Creamed Onion Bake

Creamy Vegetable Medley

(photo on page 27)

Prep Time: 15 minutes   **Cook Time:** 20 minutes

1 can (10¾ ounces) CAMPBELL'S Condensed Cream
    of Celery Soup *or* 98% Fat Free Cream of Celery
    Soup
½ cup milk
2 cups broccoli flowerets
2 medium carrots, sliced (about 1 cup)
1 cup cauliflower flowerets

1. In medium saucepan mix soup, milk, broccoli, carrots and cauliflower. Over medium heat, heat to a boil.

2. Reduce heat to low. Cover and cook 15 minutes or until vegetables are tender, stirring occasionally.   *Serves 6*

Variation: Omit milk. Substitute 1 bag (16 ounces) frozen vegetable combination (broccoli, cauliflower, carrots) for fresh vegetables.

Slim & Savory Vegetables

(photo on page 57)
Prep Time: 10 minutes   **Cook Time:** 10 minutes

**1 can (14½ ounces) SWANSON Chicken Broth
(1¾ cups)
3 cups cut-up vegetables***

1. In medium saucepan mix broth and vegetables. Over medium-high heat, heat to a boil.

2. Reduce heat to low. Cover and cook 5 minutes or until vegetables are tender-crisp. Drain.   *Serves 4*

*Use a combination of broccoli flowerets, cauliflower flowerets, carrots and celery cut in 2-inch pieces.

Note: 0g fat per serving (traditional steamed vegetable recipe with butter: 3g fat per serving)

Garlic Slim & Savory Vegetables: Substitute 1 can (14½ ounces) SWANSON Seasoned Chicken Broth with Roasted Garlic for Chicken Broth.

Broth Seasoned Rice: Reserve broth after vegetables are cooked (1½ cups). In medium saucepan over medium-high heat, heat broth to a boil. Add *½ cup* uncooked regular white rice. Cook according to package directions. *Serves 3*

Tip

Substitute 1 bag (16 ounces) frozen vegetable combination (broccoli, cauliflower, carrots) for fresh vegetables.

COLD WEATHER COMFORTS

Best Ever Meatloaf

Prep Time: 10 minutes   **Cook Time:** 1 hour 20 minutes

> 1 can (10¾ ounces) CAMPBELL'S Condensed Tomato Soup
> 2 pounds ground beef
> 1 pouch CAMPBELL'S Dry Onion Soup and Recipe Mix
> ½ cup dry bread crumbs
> 1 egg, beaten
> ¼ cup water

1. Mix *½ cup* tomato soup, beef, onion soup mix, bread crumbs and egg **thoroughly.** In baking pan shape **firmly** into 8- by 4-inch loaf.

2. Bake at 350°F. for 1¼ hours or until meat loaf is no longer pink (160°F.).

3. In small saucepan mix **2 tablespoons** drippings, remaining tomato soup and water. Heat through. Serve with meat loaf.

Serves 8

Top to bottom: *Skinny Garlic Mashed Potatoes (page 31) and Best Ever Meatloaf*

Baked Macaroni & Cheese

Prep Time: 20 minutes   **Cook Time:** 20 minutes

1 can (10¾ ounces) CAMPBELL'S Condensed
    Cheddar Cheese Soup
½ soup can milk
⅛ teaspoon pepper
2 cups hot cooked corkscrew *or* medium shell
    macaroni (about 1½ cups uncooked)
1 tablespoon dry bread crumbs
2 teaspoons margarine *or* butter, melted

1. In 1-quart casserole mix soup, milk, pepper and macaroni.

2. Mix bread crumbs with margarine and sprinkle over macaroni mixture.

3. Bake at 400°F. for 20 minutes or until hot.   *Serves 4*

To Double Recipe: Double all ingredients, except increase margarine to 1 tablespoon, use 2-quart casserole and increase baking time to 25 minutes.

Variation: Substitute 2 cups hot cooked elbow macaroni (about 1 cup uncooked) for corkscrew *or* shell macaroni.

Baked Macaroni & Cheese

No-Guilt Chicken Pot Pie

Prep Time: 10 minutes   **Cook Time:** 30 minutes

1 can (10¾ ounces) CAMPBELL'S Condensed 98%
    Fat Free Cream of Chicken Soup
1 package (about 9 ounces) frozen mixed
    vegetables, thawed (about 2 cups)
1 cup cubed cooked chicken
½ cup milk
1 egg
1 cup reduced fat all-purpose baking mix

1. Preheat oven to 400°F. In 9-inch pie plate mix soup, vegetables and chicken.

2. Mix milk, egg and baking mix. Pour over chicken mixture. Bake 30 minutes or until golden.

Serves 4

No-Guilt Turkey Pot Pie: Substitute 1 cup cubed cooked turkey for chicken.

Tip

For a variation, substitute CAMPBELL'S Condensed Cream of Chicken Soup **or** Cream of Chicken Soup with Herbs.

No-Guilt Chicken Pot Pie

Miracle Lasagna

Prep Time: 5 minutes   **Cook Time:** 1 hour
Stand Time: 5 minutes

1 jar (28 ounces) PREGO Traditional Pasta Sauce
6 *uncooked* lasagna noodles
1 container (15 ounces) ricotta cheese
8 ounces shredded mozzarella cheese (2 cups)
¼ cup grated Parmesan cheese

1. In 2-quart shallow baking dish (11- by 7-inch) spread *1 cup* pasta sauce. Top with *3 uncooked* lasagna noodles, ricotta cheese, *1 cup* mozzarella cheese, Parmesan cheese and *1 cup* pasta sauce. Top with remaining *3 uncooked* lasagna noodles and remaining pasta sauce. **Cover.**

2. Bake at 375°F. for 1 hour. Uncover and top with remaining mozzarella cheese. Let stand 5 minutes.   *Serves 6*

Meat or Mushroom Miracle Lasagna: Use 3-quart shallow baking dish (13- by 9-inch). Proceed as in Step 1. Top Parmesan cheese with 1 pound ground beef *or* sausage, cooked and drained, *or* 2 cups sliced fresh mushrooms *or* 2 jars (4½ ounces *each*) sliced mushrooms, drained.

Tip

For a variation, substitute PREGO Pasta Sauce with Fresh Mushrooms *or* PREGO Italian Sausage & Garlic Pasta Sauce.

Miracle Lasagna

Baked Ziti Supreme

Prep Time: 25 minutes   **Cook Time:** 30 minutes

    1 **pound ground beef**
    1 **medium onion, chopped (about ½ cup)**
    1 **jar (28 ounces) PREGO Pasta Sauce with Fresh**
       Mushrooms
1½ **cups shredded mozzarella cheese (6 ounces)**
    5 **cups hot cooked medium tube-shaped macaroni**
       (about 3 cups uncooked)
 ¼ **cup grated Parmesan cheese**

1. In large saucepan over medium-high heat, cook beef and onion until beef is browned, stirring to separate meat. Pour off fat.

2. Stir in pasta sauce, *1 cup* mozzarella cheese and macaroni. Spoon into 3-quart shallow baking dish. Sprinkle with remaining mozzarella cheese and Parmesan cheese. Bake at 350°F. for 30 minutes.

Serves 6

Tip

A salad of mixed greens and hot toasted garlic bread team perfectly with this quick and easy casserole.

Baked Ziti Supreme

Beef & Mozzarella Bake

Prep Time: 15 minutes   **Cook Time:** 25 minutes

   1 **pound ground beef**
   1 **can (11⅛ ounces) CAMPBELL'S Condensed Italian Tomato Soup**
   1 **can (10¾ ounces) CAMPBELL'S Condensed Cream of Mushroom Soup**
1¼ **cups water**
   1 **teaspoon dried basil leaves, crushed**
  ¼ **teaspoon pepper**
  ⅛ **teaspoon garlic powder** *or* **1 clove garlic, minced**
1½ **cups shredded mozzarella cheese (6 ounces)**
   4 **cups hot cooked medium shell macaroni (about 3 cups uncooked)**

1. In medium skillet over medium-high heat, cook beef until browned, stirring to separate meat. Pour off fat.

2. Add soups, water, basil, pepper, garlic powder, *1 cup* cheese and macaroni. Spoon into 2-quart shallow baking dish. Bake at 400°F. for 20 minutes or until hot.

3. Stir. Sprinkle remaining cheese over beef mixture. Bake 5 minutes more or until cheese is melted.
                                                 Serves 6

Variation: Substitute 4 cups hot cooked elbow macaroni (about 2 cups uncooked) for shell macaroni.

Beef & Mozzarella Bake

Beefy Macaroni Skillet

Prep Time: 10 minutes   **Cook Time:** 15 minutes

    1 pound ground beef
    1 medium onion, chopped (about ½ cup)
    1 can (10¾ ounces) CAMPBELL'S Condensed Tomato
        Soup
    ¼ cup water
    1 tablespoon Worcestershire sauce
    ½ cup shredded Cheddar cheese (2 ounces)
    2 cups cooked corkscrew macaroni (about 1½ cups
        uncooked)

1. In medium skillet over medium-high heat, cook beef and onion until beef is browned, stirring to separate meat. Pour off fat.

2. Add soup, water, Worcestershire, cheese and macaroni. Reduce heat to low and heat through.   *Serves 4*

Variation: Substitute 2 cups cooked elbow macaroni (about 1 cup uncooked) for corkscrew macaroni.

Tip

This one-skillet family-pleaser works perfectly as a busy weekday or casual weekend meal.

Beefy Macaroni Skillet

Stroganoff-Style Chicken

Prep Time: 15 minutes   **Cook Time:** 25 minutes

2 tablespoons vegetable oil
1 pound skinless, boneless chicken breasts, cut into strips
2 cups sliced mushrooms (about 6 ounces)
1 medium onion, chopped (about ½ cup)
1 can (10¾ ounces) CAMPBELL'S HEALTHY REQUEST Condensed Cream of Chicken Soup
½ cup plain nonfat yogurt
¼ cup water
4 cups hot cooked medium egg noodles (about 3 cups uncooked), cooked without salt
Paprika

1. In medium skillet over medium-high heat, heat *half* the oil. Add chicken in 2 batches and cook until browned, stirring often. Set chicken aside.

2. Reduce heat to medium. Add remaining oil. Add mushrooms and onion and cook until tender.

3. Add soup, yogurt and water. Heat to a boil. Return chicken to pan and heat through. Serve over noodles. Sprinkle with paprika.

Serves 4

Nutritional Values per Serving: Calories 499, Total Fat 14g, Saturated Fat 3g, Cholesterol 132mg, Sodium 394mg, Total Carbohydrate 53g, Protein 38g

Stroganoff-Style Chicken

Autumn Pork Chops

Prep Time: 5 minutes   **Cook Time:** 25 minutes

  1 tablespoon vegetable oil
  4 pork chops, ¾ inch thick (about 1½ pounds)
  1 can (10¾ ounces) **CAMPBELL'S** Condensed Cream
     of Celery Soup *or* 98% Fat Free Cream of Celery
     Soup
  ½ cup apple juice *or* water
  2 tablespoons spicy brown mustard
  1 tablespoon honey
     Generous dash pepper

1. In medium skillet over medium-high heat, heat oil. Add chops and cook 10 minutes or until browned. Set chops aside. Pour off fat.

2. Add soup, apple juice, mustard, honey and pepper. Heat to a boil. Return chops to pan. Reduce heat to low. Cover and cook 10 minutes or until chops are no longer pink.   *Serves 4*

Tip

You can store uncooked fresh pork tightly wrapped in butcher paper in the refrigerator up to four or five days. Freeze uncooked pork for up to one month.

Clockwise from left: *Scalloped Potato-Onion Bake (page 61),*
Slim & Savory Vegetables (page 39)
and Autumn Pork Chop

Savory Chicken Stew

Prep Time: 15 minutes   **Cook Time:** 35 minutes

1 tablespoon vegetable oil
1 pound skinless, boneless chicken breasts, cut into 1-inch pieces
1 can (10¾ ounces) CAMPBELL'S Condensed Cream of Chicken & Broccoli Soup
½ cup milk
⅛ teaspoon pepper
4 small red potatoes (about ¾ pound), cut into quarters
2 medium carrots, sliced (about 1 cup)
1 cup broccoli flowerets

1. In medium skillet over medium-high heat, heat oil. Add chicken in 2 batches and cook until browned, stirring often. Set chicken aside. Pour off fat.

2. Add soup, milk, pepper, potatoes, carrots and broccoli. Heat to a boil. Reduce heat to low. Cover and cook 15 minutes, stirring occasionally.

3. Return chicken to pan. Cover and cook 5 minutes or until chicken is no longer pink and vegetables are tender, stirring occasionally.

Serves 4

Top to bottom: *Homestyle Beef Stew (page 60) and Savory Chicken Stew*

Homestyle Beef Stew

(photo on page 59)

Prep Time: 10 minutes   **Cook Time:** 2 hours 15 minutes

> 2 tablespoons all-purpose flour
> ⅛ teaspoon pepper
> 1 pound beef for stew, cut into 1-inch cubes
> 1 tablespoon vegetable oil
> 1 can (10½ ounces) CAMPBELL'S Condensed Beef Broth
> ½ cup water
> ½ teaspoon dried thyme leaves, crushed
> 1 bay leaf
> 3 medium carrots (about ½ pound), cut into 1-inch pieces
> 2 medium potatoes (about ½ pound), cut into quarters

1. Mix flour and pepper. Coat beef with flour mixture.

2. In Dutch oven over medium-high heat, heat oil. Add beef and cook until browned, stirring often. Set beef aside. Pour off fat.

3. Add broth, water, thyme and bay leaf. Heat to a boil. Return beef to pan. Reduce heat to low. Cover and cook 1½ hours.

4. Add carrots and potatoes. Cover and cook 30 minutes more or until beef is fork-tender, stirring occasionally. Discard bay leaf.

Serves 4

Scalloped Potato-Onion Bake

(photo on page 57)

Prep Time: 15 minutes   **Cook Time:** 1 hour 15 minutes

> 1 can (10¾ ounces) CAMPBELL'S Condensed Cream of Celery Soup *or* 98% Fat Free Cream of Celery Soup
> ½ cup milk
> Dash pepper
> 4 medium potatoes (about 1¼ pounds), thinly sliced
> 1 small onion, thinly sliced (about ¼ cup)
> 1 tablespoon margarine *or* butter
> Paprika

1. Mix soup, milk and pepper. In 1½-quart casserole layer *half* the potatoes, onion and soup mixture. Repeat layers. Dot with margarine. Sprinkle with paprika.

2. Cover and bake at 400°F. for 1 hour. Uncover and bake 15 minutes more or until potatoes are tender.   *Serves 6*

Tip

For a variation and dash of color, add ¼ cup chopped fresh parsley in step 1.

Skinny Potato Soup

Prep Time: 15 minutes   **Cook Time:** 30 minutes

> 1 can (14½ ounces) SWANSON Chicken Broth (1¾ cups)
> ⅛ teaspoon pepper
> 4 green onions, sliced (about ½ cup)
> 1 stalk celery, sliced (about ½ cup)
> 3 medium potatoes (about 1 pound), peeled and sliced ¼ inch thick
> 1½ cups milk

1. In medium saucepan mix broth, pepper, onions, celery and potatoes. Over high heat, heat to a boil. Reduce heat to low. Cover and cook 15 minutes or until vegetables are tender. Remove from heat.

2. In blender or food processor, place **half** the broth mixture and ¾ **cup** milk. Cover and blend until smooth. Repeat with remaining broth mixture and remaining milk. Return to pan. Over medium heat, heat through.   *Serves 5*

Note: 2g fat per serving (traditional vichyssoise recipe: 15g fat per serving)

Tip

In warm weather, serve Chilled Skinny Potato Soup.
After blending, pour soup into a serving bowl.
Refrigerate at least 2 hours.

Top to bottom: *Skinny Clam Chowder (page 65),
Quick Vegetable Soup (page 64)
and Skinny Potato Soup*

Quick Vegetable Soup

(photo on page 63)

Prep Time: 10 minutes   **Cook Time:** 20 minutes

- 2 cans (14½ ounces *each*) SWANSON Vegetable Broth
- ½ teaspoon dried basil leaves, crushed
- ¼ teaspoon garlic powder
- 1 can (about 14½ ounces) whole peeled tomatoes, cut up
- 1 package (about 9 ounces) frozen mixed vegetables (about 2 cups)
- 1 cup *uncooked* corkscrew macaroni

In medium saucepan mix broth, basil, garlic powder, tomatoes and vegetables. Over medium-high heat, heat to a boil. Stir in macaroni. Reduce heat to medium. Cook 15 minutes or until macaroni is done, stirring occasionally.   *Serves 6*

Note: 1g fat per serving

Tip

Homemade soup in just 30 minutes? SWANSON Broth makes it easy and delicious. For a variation, substitute 1 cup uncooked elbow macaroni for corkscrew macaroni.

Skinny Clam Chowder

(photo on page 63)

Prep Time: 15 minutes   **Cook Time:** 25 minutes

> 1 can (14½ ounces) SWANSON Natural Goodness™ Chicken Broth
> ¼ teaspoon dried thyme leaves, crushed
> ⅛ teaspoon pepper
> 3 medium potatoes, peeled and cut into cubes (about 3 cups)
> 1 stalk celery, sliced (about ½ cup)
> 1 medium onion, chopped (about ½ cup)
> 1½ cups milk
> 2 tablespoons all-purpose flour
> 2 cans (6½ ounces *each*) minced clams

1. In medium saucepan mix broth, thyme, pepper, potatoes, celery and onion. Over high heat, heat to a boil. Reduce heat to low. Cover and cook 15 minutes or until vegetables are tender.

2. In bowl gradually mix milk into flour until smooth. Gradually add to broth mixture. Add clams. Cook until mixture boils and thickens, stirring constantly.   *Serves 7*

Note: 2g fat per serving (traditional New England clam chowder recipe: 10g fat per serving)

TURKEY TILL IT'S GONE

Turkey Broccoli Alfredo

Prep Time: 10 minutes   **Cook Time:** 15 minutes

6 ounces *uncooked* fettuccine
1 cup fresh *or* frozen broccoli flowerets
1 can (10¾ ounces) CAMPBELL'S Condensed Cream of Mushroom Soup *or* 98% Fat Free Cream of Mushroom Soup
½ cup milk
½ cup grated Parmesan cheese
1 cup cubed cooked turkey
¼ teaspoon freshly ground pepper

1. Prepare fettuccine according to package directions. Add broccoli for last 4 minutes of cooking time. Drain.

2. In same pan mix soup, milk, cheese, turkey, pepper and fettuccine mixture and heat through, stirring occasionally.

Serves 4

Variation: Substitute 8 ounces uncooked spaghetti for fettuccine.

Turkey Broccoli Alfredo

Quick Turkey Quesadillas

Prep Time: 10 minutes   **Cook Time:** 15 minutes

1 can (10¾ ounces) CAMPBELL'S Condensed
    Cheddar Cheese Soup
½ cup PACE Thick & Chunky Salsa *or* Picante Sauce
    (Medium)
2 cups cubed cooked turkey
10 flour tortillas (8-inch)
    Fiesta Rice (recipe follows)

1. Preheat oven to 425°F.

2. In medium saucepan mix soup, salsa and turkey. Over medium heat, heat through, stirring often.

3. Place tortillas on 2 baking sheets. Top **half** of each tortilla with **⅓ cup** soup mixture. Spread to within ½ inch of edge. Moisten edges of tortilla with water. Fold over and press edges together.

4. Bake 5 minutes or until hot. Serve with Fiesta Rice.   *Serves 4*

Fiesta Rice: In medium saucepan, mix 1 can (10½ ounces) CAMPBELL'S Condensed Chicken Broth, ½ cup water and ½ cup PACE Thick & Chunky Salsa. Over medium-high heat, heat to a boil. Stir in 2 cups uncooked Minute® Original Rice. Cover and remove from heat. Let stand 5 minutes. Fluff with fork. *Serves 4*

Top to bottom: *Turkey Corn Chowder (page 91)
and Quick Turkey Quesadillas*

Turkey Stuffing Divan

Prep Time: 15 minutes   **Cook Time:** 30 minutes

> 1¼ cups boiling water
> 4 tablespoons margarine *or* butter, melted
> 4 cups PEPPERIDGE FARM Herb Seasoned Stuffing
> 2 cups cooked broccoli cuts
> 2 cups cubed cooked turkey
> 1 can (10¾ ounces) CAMPBELL'S Condensed Cream of Celery Soup *or* 98% Fat Free Cream of Celery Soup
> ½ cup milk
> 1 cup shredded Cheddar cheese (4 ounces)

1. Mix water and margarine. Add stuffing. Mix lightly.

2. Spoon into 2-quart shallow baking dish. Arrange broccoli and turkey over stuffing. In small bowl mix soup, milk and ½ *cup* cheese. Pour over broccoli and turkey. Sprinkle remaining cheese over soup mixture.

3. Bake at 350°F. for 30 minutes or until hot.   *Serves 6*

Variation: Substitute 1 can (10¾ ounces) CAMPBELL'S Condensed Cream of Chicken Soup **or** 98% Fat Free Cream of Chicken Soup for Cream of Celery Soup. Substitute 2 cups cubed cooked chicken for turkey.

Tip

For 2 cups cooked broccoli cuts use about 1 pound fresh broccoli, trimmed, cut into 1-inch pieces (about 2 cups) **or** 1 package (10 ounces) frozen broccoli cuts (2 cups).

Turkey Stuffing Divan

Turkey Asparagus Gratin

Prep Time: 20 minutes   **Cook Time:** 30 minutes

- 1 can (10¾ ounces) CAMPBELL'S Condensed Cream of Asparagus Soup
- ½ cup milk
- ¼ teaspoon onion powder
- ⅛ teaspoon pepper
- 3 cups hot cooked corkscrew macaroni (about 2½ cups uncooked)
- 1½ cups cubed cooked turkey *or* chicken
- 1½ cups cooked cut asparagus
- 1 cup shredded Cheddar *or* Swiss cheese (4 ounces)

1. In 2-quart casserole mix soup, milk, onion powder and pepper. Stir in macaroni, turkey, asparagus and **½ cup** cheese.

2. Bake at 400°F. for 25 minutes or until hot.

3. Stir. Sprinkle remaining cheese over turkey mixture. Bake 5 minutes more or until cheese is melted.   *Serves 4*

Tip

For 1½ cups cooked cut asparagus, cook ¾ pound fresh asparagus, trimmed and cut into 1-inch pieces **or** 1 package (about 9 ounces) frozen asparagus cuts.

Turkey Asparagus Gratin

Turkey Primavera

Prep Time: 10 minutes   **Cook Time:** 20 minutes

1 can (10¾ ounces) CAMPBELL'S HEALTHY REQUEST
Condensed Cream of Mushroom Soup
½ cup milk
3 tablespoons grated Parmesan cheese
¼ teaspoon garlic powder
1 bag (16 ounces) frozen vegetable combination
(broccoli, cauliflower, carrots)
2 cups cubed cooked turkey *or* chicken
4 cups hot cooked spaghetti (about 8 ounces
uncooked), cooked without salt

1. In medium saucepan mix soup, milk, cheese, garlic powder and vegetables. Over medium heat, heat to a boil. Reduce heat to low. Cover and cook 10 minutes or until vegetables are tender-crisp, stirring occasionally.

2. Add turkey and heat through. Serve over spaghetti.

Serves 4

Nutritional Values per Serving: Calories 415, Total Fat 9g, Saturated Fat 3g, Cholesterol 58mg, Sodium 466mg, Total Carbohydrate 54g, Protein 30g

Tip

No cooked turkey or chicken on hand? Substitute
2 (5-ounce) cans of SWANSON Premium Chunk
Chicken Breast or Chunk Chicken.

In this recipe, HEALTHY REQUEST creates a creamy
sauce without the fat and calories of butter and cream!

Turkey Primavera

Country Turkey Casserole

Prep Time: 20 minutes   **Cook Time:** 25 minutes

- 1 can (10¾ ounces) CAMPBELL'S Condensed Cream of Celery Soup *or* 98% Fat Free Cream of Celery Soup
- 1 can (10¾ ounces) CAMPBELL'S Condensed Cream of Potato Soup
- 1 cup milk
- ¼ teaspoon dried thyme leaves, crushed
- ⅛ teaspoon pepper
- 4 cups cooked cut-up vegetables*
- 2 cups cubed cooked turkey *or* chicken
- 4 cups prepared PEPPERIDGE FARM Herb Seasoned Stuffing

1. In 3-quart shallow baking dish mix soups, milk, thyme, pepper, vegetables and turkey. Spoon stuffing over turkey mixture.

2. Bake at 400°F. for 25 minutes or until hot.   *Serves 5*

Use a combination of green beans cut into 1-inch pieces and sliced carrots.

Tip

For prepared stuffing, heat 1¼ cups water and 4 tablespoons margarine *or* butter to a boil. Remove from heat and add 4 cups PEPPERIDGE FARM Herb Seasoned Stuffing. Mix lightly.

Country Turkey Casserole

Turkey Broccoli Twists

Prep Time: 10 minutes   **Cook Time:** 20 minutes

    3 cups *uncooked* corkscrew macaroni
    2 cups broccoli flowerets
    2 medium carrots, sliced (about 1 cup)
    1 can (10¾ ounces) CAMPBELL'S Condensed Cream
        of Broccoli Soup *or* 98% Fat Free Cream of
        Broccoli Soup
    1 can (14½ ounces) SWANSON Chicken Broth
        (1¾ cups)
    ½ teaspoon garlic powder
    ⅛ teaspoon pepper
    2 cups cubed cooked turkey
    ¼ cup grated Parmesan cheese

1. In large saucepan prepare macaroni according to package
directions, omitting salt. Add broccoli and carrots for last
5 minutes of cooking time. Drain.

2. In same pan mix soup, broth, garlic powder, pepper, turkey and
macaroni mixture. Over medium heat, heat through, stirring
occasionally. Sprinkle with cheese.   *Serves 5*

Turkey Broccoli Twists

Easy Turkey & Biscuits

Prep Time: 15 minutes   **Cook Time:** 30 minutes

- 1 can (10¾ ounces) CAMPBELL'S Condensed Cream of Celery Soup *or* 98% Fat Free Cream of Celery Soup
- 1 can (10¾ ounces) CAMPBELL'S Condensed Cream of Potato Soup
- 1 cup milk
- ¼ teaspoon dried thyme leaves, crushed
- ¼ teaspoon pepper
- 4 cups cooked cut-up vegetables*
- 2 cups cubed cooked turkey, chicken *or* ham
- 1 package (7½ *or* 10 ounces) refrigerated buttermilk biscuits (10 biscuits)

1. In 3-quart shallow baking dish mix soups, milk, thyme, pepper, vegetables and turkey.

2. Bake at 400°F. for 15 minutes or until hot.

3. Stir. Arrange biscuits over turkey mixture. Bake 15 minutes more or until biscuits are golden.

Serves 5

*Use a combination of broccoli flowerets, cauliflower flowerets and sliced carrots **or** broccoli flowerets and sliced carrots **or** broccoli flowerets, sliced carrots and peas.*

Tip

To microwave vegetables, in 2-quart shallow microwave-safe baking dish arrange vegetables and ¼ cup water. Cover. Microwave on HIGH 10 minutes.

Easy Turkey & Biscuits

Zesty Turkey & Rice

Prep Time: 5 minutes   **Cook Time:** 30 minutes

1 can (14½ ounces) SWANSON Chicken Broth
    (1¾ cups)
1 teaspoon dried basil leaves, crushed
¼ teaspoon garlic powder
¼ teaspoon hot pepper sauce
1 can (about 14½ ounces) stewed tomatoes
¾ cup *uncooked* regular long-grain white rice
1 cup frozen peas
2 cups cubed cooked turkey *or* chicken

1. In medium saucepan mix broth, basil, garlic powder, hot pepper sauce and tomatoes. Over medium-high heat, heat to a boil. Stir in rice. Reduce heat to low. Cover and cook 20 minutes.

2. Stir in peas and turkey. Cover and cook 5 minutes more or until rice is done and most of liquid is absorbed.   *Serves 4*

Note: 3g fat per serving

Tip

The "zesty" in this all-in-one dish comes from the hot pepper sauce. If your tastes run to mild, just add a dash.

Zesty Turkey & Rice

Turkey & Stuffing Bake

Prep Time: 15 minutes   **Cook Time:** 30 minutes

1 can (14½ ounces) SWANSON Chicken Broth
    (1¾ cups)
Generous dash pepper
1 stalk celery, chopped (about ½ cup)
1 small onion, coarsely chopped (about ¼ cup)
4 cups PEPPERIDGE FARM Herb Seasoned Stuffing
4 servings sliced roasted *or* deli turkey (about
    12 ounces)
1 jar (12 ounces) FRANCO-AMERICAN Slow Roast™
    Turkey Gravy

1. In medium saucepan mix broth, pepper, celery and onion. Over high heat, heat to a boil. Reduce heat to low. Cover and cook 5 minutes or until vegetables are tender. Add stuffing. Mix lightly.

2. Spoon into 2-quart shallow baking dish. Arrange turkey over stuffing. Pour gravy over turkey.

3. Bake at 350°F. for 30 minutes or until hot.   *Serves 4*

Tip

For a variation, add ½ cup chopped nuts
with the stuffing.

Turkey & Stuffing Bake

Hot Turkey Sandwiches

Prep Time: 5 minutes   **Cook Time:** 15 minutes

> 1 jar (12 ounces) FRANCO-AMERICAN Slow Roast™ Turkey Gravy
> 2 servings sliced roasted *or* deli turkey (about 6 ounces)
> 4 slices PEPPERIDGE FARM Original White Bread
> Cranberry sauce

1. In medium skillet over medium heat, heat gravy to a boil.

2. Add turkey. Reduce heat to low and heat through. Place turkey on 2 bread slices and top with remaining bread slices. Spoon gravy over sandwiches. Serve with cranberry sauce.   *Serves 2*

Hot Roast Beef Sandwiches: Substitute FRANCO-AMERICAN Slow Roast™ Beef Gravy for the turkey gravy and slices of cooked beef for the turkey.

Hot Turkey Sandwich

Barbecued Turkey Pockets

Prep Time: 10 minutes   **Cook Time:** 15 minutes

1 can (10¾ ounces) CAMPBELL'S HEALTHY REQUEST Condensed Tomato Soup
¼ cup water
2 tablespoons packed brown sugar
2 tablespoons vinegar
1 tablespoon Worcestershire sauce
1 pound thinly sliced roasted *or* deli turkey breast
3 pita breads (6-inch), cut in half, forming 2 pockets

1. In medium skillet mix soup, water, sugar, vinegar and Worcestershire. Over medium heat, heat to a boil. Reduce heat to low and cook 5 minutes.

2. Add turkey and heat through. Spoon ½ cup turkey mixture into each pita half.   *Makes 6 sandwiches*

Nutritional Values per Serving: Calories 241, Total Fat 2g, Saturated Fat 0g, Cholesterol 63mg, Sodium 433mg, Total Carbohydrate 29g, Protein 26g

Tip

Serve these flavorful pockets with a tossed salad, fresh sliced tomatoes or fresh fruit.

In this recipe, the rich flavor of HEALTHY REQUEST soup substitutes for a higher-in-sodium barbecue sauce.

Top to bottom: *Barbecued Turkey Pocket and Hearty Turkey Vegetable Soup (page 90)*

Hearty Turkey Vegetable Soup

(photo on page 89)

Prep Time: 10 minutes   **Cook Time:** 20 minutes

   3 cans (14½ ounces *each*) SWANSON Chicken Broth
      (5¼ cups)
   ½ teaspoon dried thyme leaves, crushed
   ¼ teaspoon garlic powder *or* 2 cloves garlic, minced
   2 cups frozen whole kernel corn
   1 package (about 10 ounces) frozen cut green beans
      (about 2 cups)
   1 cup cut-up canned tomatoes
   1 stalk celery, chopped (about ½ cup)
   2 cups cubed cooked turkey *or* chicken

1. In large saucepan mix broth, thyme, garlic powder, corn, beans, tomatoes and celery. Over medium-high heat, heat to a boil. Reduce heat to low. Cover and cook 5 minutes or until vegetables are tender.

2. Add turkey and heat through.   *Serves 6*

Note: 2g fat per serving

Tip

For 2 cups cubed cooked chicken, in medium saucepan over medium heat, in 4 cups of boiling water, cook 1 pound skinless, boneless chicken breasts, cubed, 5 minutes or until chicken is no longer pink.

Turkey Corn Chowder

(photo on page 69)

Prep Time: 10 minutes   **Cook Time:** 10 minutes

1 can (10¾ ounces) CAMPBELL'S Condensed Cream
    of Celery Soup *or* 98% Fat Free Cream of Celery
    Soup
1 soup can milk
½ cup PACE Picante Sauce *or* Thick & Chunky Salsa
1 can (about 8 ounces) whole kernel corn, drained
1 cup cubed cooked turkey *or* chicken
4 slices bacon, cooked and crumbled
    Shredded Cheddar cheese
    Sliced green onions

In medium saucepan mix soup, milk, picante sauce, corn, turkey
and bacon. Over medium heat, heat through, stirring occasionally.
Top with cheese, onions and additional picante sauce.   *Serves 4*

Tip

Give this rich and creamy chowder an extra flavor
accent with PEPPERIDGE FARM Flavor Blasted™
Goldfish® snacks in Extra Cheddar or Extra Nacho
varieties.

Recipe
Index

Product Index